# FROM MASS TO MISSION
Understanding the Mass and Its Significance for Our Christian Life

## LEADER'S GUIDE

## TRISH SULLIVAN VANNI

LITURGY TRAINING PUBLICATIONS

*Nihil Obstat*
Very Reverend Daniel A. Smilanic, JCD
Vicar for Canonical Services
Archdiocese of Chicago
December 16, 2015

*Imprimatur*
Very Reverend Ronald A. Hicks
Vicar General
Archdiocese of Chicago
December 16, 2015

The *Nihil Obstat* and *Imprimatur* are declarations that the material is free from doctrinal or moral error, and thus is granted permission to publish in accordance with c. 827. No legal responsibility is assumed by the grant of this permission. No implication is contained herein that those who have granted the *Nihil Obstat* and *Imprimatur* agree with the content, opinions, or statements expressed.

In fond memory of Rev. Kevin Seasoltz, OSB, who taught that our gracious God lives for giving, especially in the Eucharist.
—PSV and DAN

Excerpts from the *Lectionary for Mass for Use in the Dioceses of the United States of America, Second Typical Edition* © 1998, 1997, 1970 by the Confraternity of Christian Doctrine, Inc., Washington, DC, and are reproduced herein by license of the copyright owner. All rights reserved. No part of *Lectionary for Mass* may be reproduced in any form without permission in writing from the Confraternity of Christian Doctrine, Inc., Washington, DC.

*From Mass to Mission: Understanding the Mass and Its Significance for Our Christian Life, Leader's Guide* materials may not be photocopied, or otherwise reproduced without permission in writing from the copyright holder above, except for those pages included on the enclosed DVD. The pages found on the accompanying DVD may be reproduced only in quantities necessary for the church, school, or group purchasing the resource. They must be reproduced along with their accompanying copyright notices. The materials included on the accompanying DVD may be distributed, copied, and shared only in those quantities necessary for the church, school, or group purchasing the resource. The videos may be uploaded to your website. Reproduction of any other part of this resource for any other purpose is both illegal and unethical.

Quotations from Pope Francis, Pope Benedict XVI, and Pope John Paul II courtesy Libreria Editrice Vaticana. Used with permission.

The title of this book was inspired by *Dies Domini*, 45. The cover of this book presents a metaphorical illustration depicting that we are sent from Mass as disciples enlightened by the light of Christ.

This book was edited by Danielle A. Noe, MDIV. Christian Rocha was the production editor, Anna Manhart was the designer, and Kari Nicholls was the production artist. Juan Alberto Castillo was the designer and production artist for the materials on the DVD.

FROM MASS TO MISSION: UNDERSTANDING THE MASS AND ITS SIGNIFICANCE FOR OUR CHRISTIAN LIFE LEADER'S GUIDE © 2016 Archdiocese of Chicago: Liturgy Training Publications, 3949 South Racine Avenue, Chicago, IL 60609; 1-800-933-1800; fax 1-800-933-7094; e-mail: orders@ltp.org; website: www.LTP.org. All rights reserved.

Cover art by Martin Erspamer, OSB; interior images by Martin Erspamer, OSB 1, 6, 11, 15, 20; interior icons from Iconfinder.

20 19 18 17 16   1 2 3 4 5

Printed in the United States of America.

ISBN 978-1-61671-301-0

FMML

# CONTENTS

Welcome!   iv
    About the Participant's Booklet   iv
    Using the *Leader's Guide*   v
    Using the DVD   v
    Leading Formation Sessions with Adults   vi
    Planning, Logistics, and Advertising   viii

Chapter One: Why Go to Mass?
**Session 1 Outline** ...................................................................1

Chapter Two: The Introductory Rites
**Session 2 Outline** ...................................................................6

Chapter Three: The Liturgy of the Word
**Session 3 Outline** .................................................................11

Chapter Four: The Liturgy of the Eucharist
**Session 4 Outline** .................................................................15

Chapter Five: The Concluding Rites and Our Call to Mission
**Session 5 Outline** .................................................................20

# Welcome!

In *From Mass to Mission: Understanding the Mass and Its Significance for Our Christian Life* we read that ever since the Lord's Death and Resurrection, his followers have gathered on the Lord's Day "in small groups or large, in spaces that are soaring and grand or modest and humble, . . . to share this holy meal together. For Catholics, this is the celebration of the Mass. We leave home. We gather with friends and strangers. We enact a predictable ritual, and we change in unpredictable ways. We place all the events of the past week inside that Mass to offer them for the glory of God. We prepare for the duties of the coming week and seek their sanctification. We discard from our lives what keeps us from Christ, and we retain what makes us good disciples."

For many people, going to Sunday Mass is simply something they "do" as good Catholics. Keeping the Lord's Day holy is something they were taught as children, and attending Mass is simply matter of fact. But even if you're very committed to participating, it's easy to get out of touch with the wonder and gift of it all, and the ways in which we are changed unpredictably.

This *Leader's Guide* is a companion to the booklet *From Mass to Mission: Understanding the Mass and Its Significance for Our Christian Life* by Trish Sullivan Vanni with Paul Turner. It provides a thoughtful window into the meaning of the Mass, the theology that helps us understand it more fully, and an opportunity to become even more engaged participants in this important weekly (or daily) liturgy.

In this *Leader's Guide*, you'll find five session outlines with an opening and closing prayer, discussion sparkers, teaching points, and social media suggestions. Each session outline is tied to a video provided on the accompanying DVD. There are even materials to help you easily market *From Mass to Mission: Understanding the Mass and its Significance for Our Christian Life* in your parish—bulletin inserts, flyers, e-mails, etc. Our hope is that the rich resources of this *Leader's Guide* along with the participant book will empower you to create a wonderful experience for the adult learners with whom you are working.

Thank you for being part of passing on the beauty and meaning of the Eucharist as experienced in the Mass. This powerful sacrament is a transformative gift of sacrifice and love from our Lord Jesus Christ. May your journey with your participants not only deepen their faith, wonder, and action, but yours, as well.

—Trish Sullivan Vanni

## About the Participant's Booklet

There are a number of ways that you can use the booklet *From Mass to Mission: Understanding the Mass and Its Significance for Our Christian Life*. You can simply distribute it, encouraging people to read it and use it at home. Many people are busy or question the value of coming to a workshop or learning session, and reading on their own is appreciated.

You might consider making the booklet available in the church vestibule, pamphlet kiosk, or parish office. Consider giving copies to liturgical ministers, worship commission members, parish staff, ministers to the homebound, Christian Initiation sponsors or team members, and other adult faith sharing groups. Similarly, the book can be particularly valuable for parents of those preparing for first Communion who may need a refresher on the Eucharist. Daily Mass attendees, who already feel a deep connection, will appreciate the detail and the theological insight the booklet offers.

## Using the Leader's Guide

This *Leader's Guide* will help you to create a five-session learning experience that ties the participant's booklet to a larger group experience and deepens their personal and communal connection to the liturgy. Each of the session outlines are tied to a teaching segment on the accompanying DVD. You will be able to choose from the suggested activities to augment the learning of participants. Each session outline includes the following:

- formation/teaching objectives
- list of materials needed and preparation reminders
- video for each session
- references to DVD for supplemental materials
- opening and closing prayer
- topical teaching points
- discussion sparkers
- movie suggestions
- preparation suggestions for each session
- advertising ideas for each session
- postsession social media ideas

You can use the included sessions to build a daylong or weekend retreat, pulling together a focus that best meets the needs of those with whom you are working. By selecting activities, prayers, and more, you can provide participants with a wonderful immersion into the meaning and beauty of the Mass. Each session is designed to be no more than an hour.

Consider adding activities and segments of *From Mass to Mission* as a mystagogical experience for those who were recently initiated at the Easter Vigil. Invite their sponsors, formation ministers, and others accompanying them on their journey. Provide this opportunity during Easter Time to break open the mystery of the Mass.

These sessions can be the heart of an enrichment experience for those participating in liturgical ministries. You can also use the material to support parents and guardians as they form the children they love for first Communion. Ideas for learning and for sharing experiences with children are also incorporated in this *Leader's Guide*.

Since the Church teaches that the Eucharist is the "source and summit of the Christian life" (*Lumen gentium*, 11), you might consider incorporating these sessions into parish staff meetings or scheduling a retreat for the *entire* parish staff. Doing so will help situate the ministerial efforts of the entire parish as flowing from the Eucharist itself, thus creating welcoming, loving, and evangelizing communities.

This *Leader's Guide* provides significantly more approaches to learning, participant activities, and narrative material about the Eucharist than you'll need. You can follow each session closely or customize it to meet the particular needs or interests of your group (for example, substituting hymns with which they are familiar through the worship of your community for the contemporary hymns we suggest). You know the adults in your community best.

## Using the DVD

The DVD provided in this *Leader's Guide* includes supplemental materials for adult formation as well as PDF bulletin inserts, flyers, and letters for advertising formation opportunities for youth in the parish or school as well as connecting with parents and guardians. The PDF files are editable so that you may customize the text to your parish's needs. These files may also be posted on the parish or school website, social media page, or blog; sent by e-mail; or printed and sent by mail. The opening and closing prayers for each session are provided as separate PDFs to print and place in ritual binders. PowerPoint slides for each session and memes to post and prompt discussion on Facebook (and other social media sites) are also provided.

To access the files on the DVD you must use a computer with a DVD drive. Select "start-here" and an interactive menu will open. The files are organized on the menu in this way:

- Bulletin Inserts
- Flyers
- Letters and e-mails
- Opening and Closing Prayer
- PowerPoint Slides
- Social Media Resources
- Resources for Parent or Guardian First Communion Retreat
- Videos

## Videos

The DVD includes a series of five short videos about the Mass as well as a promotional video for parishes to use to help advertise the *From Mass to Mission* experience in your parish. Each video corresponds to the material provided in the booklet *From Mass to Mission: Understanding the Mass and Its Significance for Our Christian Life* and includes interviews with noted theologians, liturgists, and Catholics with additional information about the Mass. The videos are intended to be shown in your formation session. Suggestions for incorporating the videos are provided in each session outline in this *Leader's Guide*. You may upload the videos to your parish website, blog, or social media page. Directions for playing and uploading the videos to a website are found on the DVD (select "Videos" and then "How to Play or Upload the Videos"). The videos may be played on your computer with a DVD drive.

# Leading Formation Sessions with Adults

While adult faith formation is about content, it is even more about relationship. When you gather, you want to create a space in which participants can be at home, socialize, and connect. The following ideas will help you to create a deep experience for all involved.

## Using the Participant's Booklet at Sessions

The book, *From Mass to Mission: Understanding the Mass and Its Significance for Our Christian Life*, provides valuable information that will enable people to participate more fully in each learning session. Encourage each participant to bring their book every time they gather, and support couples in each having their own book. Participants will use the book for some of the activities. They should not shy away from writing in the book, highlighting paragraphs or single sentences that strike them, or taking notes in the margins. By doing so, they will capture some of the group learning experience and can refresh their memories down the line when they come back to the book for any reason.

## Environment

Consider setting up a prayer corner in the room in which you are meeting, with a small altar cloth in the color of the liturgical season and a table cross. Light a candle. These simple additions can convey to participants that while this is a learning experience, it is also an experience of being a community of faith.

## Hospitality

The Gospel accounts reveal to us that Jesus was quite social. An itinerant preacher and teacher, he made his way from community to community gathering his followers, often around the fellowship of meals. Connecting over food is an essential human experience, one that we honor every time we come together to participate in the Lord's Supper. Consider simple hospitality for your group. If you meet Sunday mornings after Mass, offer coffee and pastries, bagels, or doughnuts. If you meet in the evenings, offer beverages and cookies or pastries, or provide bowls of candy on the table.

## Honor the Time Commitment

Time is a precious commodity nowadays. Even if you have to stop an exercise or experience earlier than you think ideal, it is important to end on time. Many people are aware of promises to return home to spouses and children. Others may be aware that a workday is looming and they have things to prepare. Some are moving on to other obligations after your session. Respecting a start and finish time will support your group in honoring their promise to be present.

## Use Nametags

Often, our parishes are places where people pray in anonymity. Participants may find that they have friends in the room (particularly if they are part of a session for parents and guardians of a child preparing for first Communion). However, many people will know no one. Help everyone be comfortable in using and getting to know each other's names by supplying nametags.

## Electronic Devices

Start each session by respectfully asking that people turn off their phones or other devices. If they cannot do this (for example, a baby sitter might call), they should put them on silent, but please do not leave them on the table top. If they balk, observe that three world leaders—President Obama, President Hollande, and Prime Minister David Cameron—all have a no-phone policy in meetings. They are left at the door with a sticky note with the owner's name.

## Small Groups

When we are asked to place ourselves in small groups, it's completely understandable that we gravitate to friends. It's a rare person who will turn to a group of people with whom they are not well acquainted to form a discussion group. However, when we are gathered as God's people, the Church, there are no "insiders" and no "outsiders." To help people bridge their friend circles to new people, you may have to structure the discussion groups in advance. You can do this by placing numbers on their nametags or using place cards. The latter can be particularly helpful if you'd like to mix the groups up from week to week. Generally speaking, once adults take their seat and settle in, they don't like having to gather up their belongings and move.

## Affirm Confidentiality

The sessions will be livelier if participants feel that it is safe for them to express their opinions or to raise their questions. Whenever a group gathers for learning and conversation, it is helpful to set ground rules—or norms—to set expectations and shape behaviors. By making these rules explicit at the beginning of working together, the group has a sense of how to behave and the leader has a place to point to when participants stray from their agreements.

# Planning, Logistics, and Advertising

Select a coordinator or formation team to deliver *From Mass to Mission: Understanding the Mass and Its Significance for Our Christian Life*. The *From Mass to Mission* learning experience is appropriate to any season of the liturgical year, and can also be used as a special experience during Lent or for parents of children preparing for first Communion.

- Start by developing a calendar for your sessions. *From Mass to Mission* can be done in a variety of ways. It can be presented as a multiday learning experience or used to create the heart of a special morning or day-long retreat.

- Decide on dates, time, and locations with sensitivity to other activities happening in the parish and the greater community. You don't want to calendar a retreat, for example, on the weekend of the parish festival or the weekend on which Super Bowl Sunday occurs.

- There are flyer, bulletin insert, and letter and e-mail templates on the DVD for you to use to promote the experience to those you are hoping to attract.

- Purchase copies of *From Mass to Mission: Understanding the Mass and Its Significance for Our Christian Life* and distribute them to participants. You will want to have these in hands at least two weeks before you plan on meeting.

- Recruit a team who will host and facilitate the experience.
  - You may know people who already have a deep relationship with the Eucharist. For example, you could invite those who serve your parish as extraordinary ministers of Holy Communion to participate.
  - These people should be coached to be committed listeners, not participants. By this we mean that their job is to be enthusiastic welcomers, great listeners in small group (if you have enough adults to have one per group). They should be encouraged to monitor how much they share in the small groups and be encouraged to keep the space open for participants—even if that means that there is occasional silence.

- See if you can identify particular gifts or interests in your adult leaders. A parish cantor or guitarist who is comfortable leading the suggested music; a reader who would be willing to proclaim the reading during the opening prayer. Some will be super at hospitality logistics. Invite those who are sharing in this ministerial experience to contribute from their strengths as disciples. Consider putting together a list of possible ways people can contribute, like those just mentioned, to provide entry points for your adults.

- Request that parishioners RSVP so that you will know how many booklets to purchase, name tags to print, and so on.

- To distribute *From Mass to Mission: Understanding the Mass and Its Significance for Our Christian Life* you can do one of the following:
  - Mail the booklets. This will allow people to prepare in advance for the first session, something that is particularly valuable to more introverted participants.
  - Distribute the booklets to participants when they gather. If you do this, we suggest printing out two sets of label-style name tag sheets. Put one of the labels with the participants name on the back of the book. That way, the inevitably abandoned copies can find their way home.

- At least six weeks in advance, begin using your bulletin, website, and Mass announcements to make the community aware of this adult learning opportunity.

- This *Leader's Guide* provides you with promotional materials and follow-up approaches for each session you convene so that you can get them to your community in a timely manner.

# Chapter One: Why Go to Mass?
# Session 1 Outline

## Advertising before Session 1

You will need to advertise the *From Mass to Mission* experience in your parish. Consider whether you will be hosting this event as a retreat or as a series of five sessions. Bulletin inserts, flyers, and letters and e-mails are found on the DVD. Select the options for "Retreat," "Initial Promotion for Five Sessions," and "Session 1."

## Objectives

- ❖ Develop a more mature understanding of what is accomplished for humanity in the Eucharist.
- ❖ Introduce core theological principles regarding the Mass.
- ❖ The liturgy is the source and summit of our faith.
- ❖ Full, conscious, and active participation at Mass.
- ❖ See the connection between participating at Mass and participating in the world
- ❖ The structure of the Mass.

## Preparation Items

- snacks and beverages (pastries, soft drinks, coffee, water)
- hospitality minister(s) to greet people as they arrive
- name tags
- computer, screen, and projector
- DVD or Blu-ray player and TV
- Session 1 video
- PowerPoint for Session 1 (show slide #1 as people gather)
- *Babette's Feast* (optional movie)
- prayer space has been prepared
- ritual binders for opening/closing prayer
- Lectionary #68B
- music for prayer
- volunteers for leading prayer, leading music, and proclaiming the Gospel
- closing prayer
- *From Mass to Mission: Understanding the Mass and Its Significance for Our Christian Life*, chapter one

# Opening Prayer

Be sure to prepare the environment before leading this session. The session leader leads prayer. You will want to find a volunteer to proclaim the reading. Invite a parish cantor (and instrumentalist, if possible) to lead all in an opening song about discipleship that is familiar to your parishioners. Suggestions are "I Heard the Voice of Jesus Say" (KINGSFOLD), "Come to Me" by J. Michael Joncas (GIA Publications), "Bring Forth the Kingdom" by Marty Haugen (GIA Publications), "We Will Serve the Lord" by Rory Cooney (GIA Publications), "The Servant Song" by Richard Gillard (GIA Publications), or "As a Fire Is Meant for Burning" (BEACH SPRING). Make sure enough hymnals or song sheets (be sure to secure proper copyright permission) are in place for all to participate. You might consider printing the PDF of the opening prayer and place it in a ritual binder for both the leader and the reader. The opening prayer for Session 1 is found on the DVD. Or the reader may use Lectionary #68B. Place the binder or Lectionary on a podium before prayer for the reader.

*Invite all to stand and sing the opening song.*

**Leader:** In the name of the Father, † and of the Son, and of the Holy Spirit.

**All:** Amen.

**Reader:** A reading from the holy Gospel according to Mark.     *1:14–20*

**All:** Glory to you, O Lord.

*All make the Sign of the Cross on their forehead, lips, and heart.*

> After John had been arrested, Jesus came to Galilee proclaiming the gospel of God: "This is the time of fulfillment. The kingdom of God is at hand. Repent, and believe in the gospel."
>
> As he passed by the Sea of Galilee, he saw Simon and his brother Andrew casting their nets into the sea; they were fishermen. Jesus said to them, "Come after me, and I will make you fishers of men." Then they abandoned their nets and followed him. He walked along a little farther and saw James, the son of Zebedee, and his brother John. They too were in a boat mending their nets. Then he called them. So they left their father Zebedee in the boat along with the hired men and followed him.

**Reader:** The Gospel of the Lord.

**All:** Praise to you, Lord Jesus Christ.

*Everyone may be seated. Invite participants to reflect on the Gospel in small groups. Ask: What does it mean to follow Jesus? How is this call connected to the Mass? Invite the small groups to share with the larger group. Then conclude the opening prayer and reflection with the prayer below.*

**Leader:** Loving God,
    we thank you for the time we have together
    and the gift of one another.
    Soften our hearts that we may more fully feel
      your love for us.
    Open our ears so that we can hear in new
      ways about the gift of the Eucharist.
    Help us know you so well that
      we are confident
    in carrying your message of hope and love to
      the world.
    Through Christ our Lord.

**All:** Amen.

**Leader:** In the name of the Father, † and of the Son, and of the Holy Spirit.

**All:** Amen.

# Discussions and Reflections

## Reflection on Chapter One

In small groups, ask participants to share their reactions to chapter one in *From Mass to Mission* by Trish Sullivan Vanni. Slide #2 in the PowerPoint for Session 1 includes these discussion sparkers: What struck you? What was new to you? What inspired you? Invite participants to share their reflections with the larger group. Other questions are found in the booklet on page 10.

## The Importance of Mass and Video

Break into small groups. Before showing the video for chapter one, show slide #3 and ask the following question: Why do you go to Mass? Why do you think going to Mass is important? Discuss as a small group. Show the video for Session 1. After watching the video, show slide #4 and ask: What is your reaction to the ideas presented in the video? Which do you find compelling? Which does your parish live out well in their celebrations of the Mass? What areas could be improved? After the discussion, invite the smaller groups to share with the larger group.

## Liturgy as Source and Summit

In order to understand the Mass more fully, we need to understand its importance and place in the life of the Church. The video you just watched offered insight into the ways Catholics understand the Eucharist. Show slide #5 and refer to the booklet, page 8. Note that the *Constitution on the Sacred Liturgy* was the first document of the Second Vatican Council. This document sets the stage for all post-Conciliar liturgical theology and teaches that "the liturgy is the summit toward which the activity of the Church is directed; at the same time it is the fount from which all the Church's power flows" (10). This powerful statement places the Eucharist in the heart of the Church's life (a similar quote is included in *Lumen gentium*, 11, as noted in the booklet on page 8).

Show slide #6 and ask: Have you ever reached a summit? What was it like? What does that image evoke for you when you think of the Eucharist? After the discussion, invite the smaller groups to share with the larger group. Then show slide #7 and ask: Have you ever come to a fountain? What made that memorable? What does that image for the Eucharist evoke? How does this relate to the Mass? How is the Mass both the source and summit of your own life? After the discussion, invite the smaller groups to share with the larger group.

## Full, Conscious, and Active Participation

Refer to page 8 in the booklet. Emphasize that participating at Mass is the most important act that Catholics do and it involves certain responsibilities that come from our Baptism, including active participation. Show slide #8 in the PowerPoint. Again, we hear from the *Constitution on the Sacred Liturgy*. Read the quote: "The Church earnestly desires that all the faithful be led to that full, conscious, and active participation in liturgical celebrations called for by the very nature of the liturgy. Such participation by the Christian people as 'a chosen race, a royal priesthood, a holy nation, God's own people' (1 Peter 2:9; see cf. 2:4–5), is their right and duty by reason of their baptism" (14).

Show slide #9 and ask small groups: What does "full, conscious, and active participation" mean to you? Do you participate actively in the Mass? Why or why not? Why is participating at Mass important? What do you need, or need to let go of, in order to do better? Is there a connection between participating at Mass and participating in the world? Why or why not? How? After the discussion, invite the smaller groups to share with the larger group.

## Eucharist as Meal

Refer to page 1 in the booklet and show slide #10. Read the passage from Matthew 26. Emphasize that we gather in memory of Jesus. Before embracing his Passion and Death, Jesus gathered his disciples and instituted this holy meal. He took the bread and said the blessing, broke the bread, and shared it; he took a cup of wine, blessed it, and shared it. His promise was that whenever this was done in remembrance of him, he would be there, and his followers would become one body in him.

Show slide #11. For many of us, the natural connection between our communal celebration of the Eucharist and the family meal has been eroded. The Eucharist is a sacrifice, and it is also a meal, and it is challenging to confer the importance of the latter in an age where there is a breakdown in the family meal. Many young people grab meals on the fly, or eat by themselves at a kitchen counter or in front of the television. The family meal has traditionally been a place to come together, share about the day, discuss news and generally reconnect. The Catholic Mass is a sacrifice and it also is a fellowship meal. Encourage adults to consider making dinner for their family one day this week, gathering people at a table with a nice setting, including a candle, and a prayer of thanksgiving.

Refer to slide #11 and ask: What challenges dinner time for you? Have you ever connected your experience at home around a meal to that of gathering for the Eucharist? After the discussion, invite the smaller groups to share with the larger group.

## The Parts of the Mass

Show slide #12. Note the repetitious nature of the Mass:
- The Introductory Rites
- The Liturgy of the Word
- The Liturgy of the Eucharist
- The Concluding Rites

Show slide #13 and ask: Prior to this session, did you know that the Mass has four parts? Are there parts of the Mass that grab and keep your attention? Parts that cause you to lose your focus? What are they? Why do some parts keep your focus? After the discussion, invite the smaller groups to share with the larger group.

Note that at the next session we will focus on the meaning of the Introductory Rites.

## Final Discussion

Show slide #14 and ask small groups to discuss these questions: How are you relating to what you are learning and reflecting on about the Mass? Do you see this as an opportunity to change your understanding of the Mass? How does what you are learning today differ from what you were taught as a child?

## Optional Movie

If your session is taking place within a longer retreat, you might consider showing the movie *Babette's Feast* (G) followed by large group discussion. This Danish film won the Academy Award for "Best Foreign Language Film" in 1997. *Babette's Feast* is about austerity and celebration, solitude and community, and so much more. A film with strong Eucharistic themes, it could be shown followed by discussion as part of your retreat, if time allows.

# Preparing for the Next Session

Mass is so much more than a "Sunday obligation." Read this quote from a 2014 General Audience with Pope Francis (aloud and slowly): "Dear friends, we don't ever thank the Lord enough for the gift he has given us in the Eucharist! It is a very great gift, and that is why it is so important to go to Mass on Sunday. Go to Mass not just to pray, but to receive Communion, the bread that is the Body of Jesus Christ who saves us, forgives us, and unites us to the Father. It is a beautiful thing to do!"

At the end of the session say: This week, note which events in your life seem most significant, gathering them to bring with you next Sunday. See if you find connections between your experiences and what is available in Mass. Participants may also reflect on the questions found on page 19 in their booklet. Ask them to bring their reflections to the next session and read chapter two in *From Mass to Mission*.

Tell participants to check out the parish Facebook page for an online discussion (see below under Social Media).

# Closing Prayer

The closing prayer is found on PowerPoint slide #15 and in the PDF for the opening and closing prayer.

**Leader:** We close with a prayer from St. Ephrem of Syria, a deacon, writer of hymns, and theologian of the fourth century. His hymns were written to provide catechesis, and some even warn against heresies. Let us pray together:

Open your heart,
learn in detail
his sufferings
and say to yourself:
God who is without sin
today was given up,
today was mocked,
today was abused,
today was struck,
today was scourged,
today wore
a crown of thorns,
today was crucified,
he, the heavenly Lamb.
Amen.

# Advertising the Next Session

Bulletin inserts, flyers, letters and e-mails are found on the DVD. You will need to send those for Session 2.

# Social Media Discussion

Social media is a good way to continue online conversations after your session or retreat, build community, and encourage other parishioners to attend the next session. Post any of the following memes and discussion sparkers on the parish Facebook page. The memes may also be posted on Pinterest and Twitter. They are found on the DVD (click on "Social Media Resources").

- Upload Meme 1A with this status message: *Did you go to Mass this weekend? Why? What brings you there? What holds you to that practice? Has anything ever intruded on that commitment?* **#masstomission**

- Upload Meme 1B with this status message: *What does it mean to be openhearted? Why is that a quality we bring to Mass?* **#masstomission**

- Upload Meme 1C with this status message: *What do you remember about your first Communion? What made that day special for you and important to your family and community?* **#masstomission**

- Upload Meme 1D with this status message: *Are you tolerant of mystery? Is it easy for you to dwell in it? What do you think helps people experience mystery? What impedes this experience?* **#masstomission**

- Upload Meme 1E with this status message: *As you drive or walk to Mass, imagine the great "cloud of witnesses" (Hebrews 12:1) that have gone before you in faith. Who stands out to you? Why?* **#masstomission**

- With your smart phone, take a picture of the front door of your church with this status message: *Waiting to be opened for you.* **#masstomission**

# Chapter Two: The Introductory Rites

# Session 2 Outline

## Objectives

- Understand that gathering is a liturgical act and an important part of the Mass.
- See singing and moving in sacred space as acts of worship.
- Gain insight into the Penitential Act, Kyrie, and Gloria.

## Preparation Items

- snacks and beverages (pastries, soft drinks, coffee, water)
- hospitality minister(s) to greet people as they arrive
- name tags
- computer, screen, and projector
- DVD or Blu-ray player and TV
- Session 2 video
- PowerPoint for Session 2 (show slide #1 as people gather)
- *50 First Dates* (optional movie)
- prayer space has been prepared
- ritual binders for opening/closing prayer
- Lectionary #58A
- music for prayer
- volunteers for leading music and proclaiming the Gospel
- hymnals or song sheets for the opening song
- copies of the parish bulletin and local newspaper
- *The Sound of Music, Ghandi, Backdraft, Fiddler on the Roof*
- bowl with blessed water
- *From Mass to Mission: Understanding the Mass and Its Significance for Our Christian Life,* chapter two
- flip chart, wipe off board, or white board

## Opening Prayer

Be sure to prepare the environment before leading this session. The session leader leads prayer. You will want to find a volunteer to proclaim the reading. Invite a parish cantor (and guitarist) to lead all in an opening song about gathering that is familiar to your parishioners. Suggestions are "Gathered as One" by Paul Tate (WLP), "Gather Us In" by Marty Haugen (GIA), or "Gather Your People, O Lord" by Bob Hurd (OCP). You might consider printing the PDF of the opening prayer and placing it in a ritual binder for both the leader and the reader. The opening prayer for Session 1 is found on the DVD. Or the reader may use Lectionary #58A. Place the binder or Lectionary on a podium before prayer for the reader.

*Invite all to stand and sing the opening song.*

**Leader:** In the name of the Father, † and of the Son, and of the Holy Spirit.

**All:** Amen.

**Reader:** A reading from the holy Gospel according to Matthew.  *28:16–20*

The eleven disciples went to Galilee, to the mountain to which Jesus had ordered them. When they saw him, they worshiped, but they doubted. Then Jesus approached and said to them, "All power in heaven and on earth has been given to me. Go, therefore, and make disciples of all nations, baptizing them in the name of the Father, and of the Son, and of the Holy Spirit, teaching them to observe all that I have commanded you. And behold, I am with you always, until the end of the age."

**Reader:** The Gospel of the Lord.

**All:** Praise to you, Lord Jesus Christ.

*Everyone may be seated. Invite participants to reflect on the Gospel in small groups. Ask: Think about your Baptism. Why is it an important responsibility of our baptismal call to worship? How do we respond to our Baptismal call in the world? What does today's Gospel tell us about our call? How is this related to Mass? Invite the small groups to share with the larger group. Then conclude the opening prayer and reflection with the payer below.*

**Leader:** Lord Jesus, life is full.
Sometimes it's joyful and sometimes
  it's a strain.
At times we feel connected and at other times
  we feel alone.
Be with us tonight,
and help us learn to remember
that "Bidden or unbidden, God is present."[1]

Help us remember that we are surrounded by
  your love and forgiveness.
You live and reign for ever.

**All:** Amen.

**Leader:** In the name of the Father, † and of the Son, and of the Holy Spirit.

**All:** Amen.

# Discussions and Reflections

## Reflection on Chapter Two

In small groups, ask participants to share their reactions to chapter two in *From Mass to Mission*. Slide #2 in the PowerPoint for Session 2 includes these discussion sparkers: What struck you? What was new to you? What inspired you? Invite participants to share their reflections with the larger group. Other questions are found in the booklet on page 19.

## The Introductory Rites and Video

Show slides #3 and #4. Read the quote from the *General Instruction of the Roman Missal* (the document which provides instructions for celebrating the Mass) stating the purpose of the Introductory Rites: "Their purpose is to ensure that the faithful, who have come together as one, establish communion and dispose themselves properly to listen to the Word of God and to celebrate the Eucharist worthily" (46). Show slide #4 and note the different parts of the Introductory Rite.

Show the video for Session 2. After watching the video, show slide #5 and ask: What is your reaction to the ideas presented in the video? Which do you find compelling? Which does your parish live out well in their celebration of the Mass? What areas could be improved? Then show slide #7 and ask: How well do you prepare yourself for Mass? What could you do, or what do you need to do to make it easier to prepare both externally

---

1 Attributed to Desiderius Erasmus.

and internally? Invite the smaller groups to share with the larger group.

## Gathering

The video you just watched offered insight into the ways Catholics understand the Introductory Rites of the Mass. Slides #8, #9, and #10 include the following quotation from Alexander Schmemann. Say: Alexander Schmemann was an Eastern Orthodox priest and theologian. In his work, *For the Life of the World,* he reflects on the importance of gathering for Mass. Read the quote slowly to allow adults to read the quote while you say it aloud:

> "The journey begins when Christians leave their homes and beds. They leave, indeed, their life in this present and concrete world, and whether they have to drive fifteen miles or walk a few blocks, a sacramental act is already taking place, an act which is the very condition of everything else that is to happen. For they are now on their way to *constitute the Church,* or to be more exact, to be transformed into the Church of God. They have been individuals, some white, some black, some poor, some rich, they have been the 'natural' world and a natural community. And now they have been called to 'come together in one place,' to bring their lives, their very 'world' with them and to be more than what they were: a *new* community with a new life. We are already far beyond the categories of common worship and prayer. The purpose of this 'coming together' is not simply to add a religious dimension to the natural community, to make it 'better'—more responsible, more Christian. The purpose is to *fulfill the Church,* and that means to make present the One in whom all things are at their *end,* and all things are at their *beginning*."[2]

Continue to display the slides, and say to the small groups: Read the excerpt from Alexander Schmemann out loud again in your small group. As you read it, think about one or two words that seem meaningful to you. Write down these words. Compare what you wrote. Why did you choose the words or phrases you chose? Show the previous slides if participants need to refer to the quote.

## Procession

For this exercise, you will need computers or DVD/Blu-Ray players and a TV for each group. Assign each group a video to watch from the options listed below. Have them work with the questions. Ask that one person in the group scribe the answers and that another person be the reporter who will share their work with the large group. Say: Watch your movie clip with your group. Show slide #11. Ask the group to discuss the following: How does the procession fit into the ritual of the day (wedding, funeral)? What are people wearing? How are they moving? What values or themes does the procession communicate? What does a procession add to the experience for the people processing? What does it add for those witnessing the procession? Show slide #12 and ask: How does what you notice illuminate the processions at Mass (the Entrance and the Communion procession, the procession with the *Book of the Gospels,* the procession to receive Communion)?

Wedding Procession from *The Sound of Music* (movie with Julie Andrews) (Scene: 2 hours and 15 minutes into the film)

Wedding Procession from *The Sound of Music Live!* (NBC live production with Carrie Underwood) (Scene: 1 hour and 44 minutes into the film)

Wedding Procession from *Fiddler on the Roof* (Scene: 1 hour and 30 minutes into the film)

Funeral Procession from *Ghandi* (Scene: 4 minutes into the film)

Funeral Procession from *Backdraft* (Scene: 2 hours and 3 minutes into the film)

---

2  Alexander Schmemann, *For the Life of the World* (Crestwood: St. Vladimir's Seminary Press, 1973), 27.

## Penitential Act

Show slide #13 and state the meaning of the Penitential Act. Essentially, the Penitential Act expresses, in a communal setting, our need for God's mercy. We are all sinners needing forgiveness and needing to forgive. Show slide #14 and ask the following: When was the last time you thought about sin? Do you believe sin exists? What do you think is more important: the cause of sin or the results from sin? When is the last time you went to reconciliation? Why is it significant that the Mass includes prayers in which we ask God to forgive our sin? In what ways does it praise God? How do you experience God's mercy? How is the Penitential Act at Mass different from receiving the Sacrament of Reconciliation?

## Activity Four: the Gloria

The Gloria is an ancient hymn. Its origins come from the Scriptural account of the angels to the shepherds in the Gospel according to Luke. The Gloria gives us many words to give praise to God. Our minds and hearts are overwhelmed with wonder for God, and we cannot possibly say or sing our praise with a just few words. The Gloria gives us this opportunity to praise God with a litany of words and phrases.

Slow slide #15 and ask: In what ways do you give God glory? Where in your ordinary day do you find examples of God's glory? In what ways are you excited about God? What is your experience of singing the Gloria at Mass?

## Optional Movie

If your session is taking place within a longer retreat, you might consider showing the movie, *50 First Dates* (PG-13) followed by large group discussion. In this film, Harry falls in love with Lucy, but finds out that she has severe short-term memory loss. Every day, she can't remember what happened the day before. Every morning, the determined Harry tries to woo her again. This movie should provoke a great conversation about commitment, our willingness to come to situations with complete freshness, faithfulness, hope, and more. You might consider showing this movie if your session is a longer retreat.

## Preparing for the Next Session

Encourage participants to take a look at this week's parish bulletin and see what readings are scheduled for next Sunday. If they are not printed there, you can find them on the website of the United States Conference of Catholic Bishops (http://www.usccb.org/). Read them early in the week, and consider praying with them. See if awareness of them colors any aspect of your life as you journey through each day. Parishes should consider offering participants a resource that includes reflections on the Sunday Gospel, such as LTP's *Sunday Prayer for Catholics* or, for families, LTP's *Celebrating Sunday for Catholic Families*. Also encourage participants to notice where there is silence in the Mass. Participants may also reflect on the questions found on page 27 in their booklet. Ask them to bring their reflections to the next session and read chapter three in *From Mass to Mission*.

## Closing Prayer

Pray the Confiteor to close your session. You may print and place it in a ritual binder. It's found on the DVD. Select the opening and closing prayer for Session 2. It's also found on slide #16.

**Leader:** I confess to almighty God

**All:** and to you, my brothers and sisters,
that I have greatly sinned,
in my thoughts and in my words,
in what I have done and in what I have failed to do;
through my fault,
through my fault,
through my most grievous fault;
therefore, I ask blessed Mary, ever-virgin,
all the Angels and Saints,
and you, my brothers and sisters,
to pray for me to the Lord our God.
Amen.

## Advertising the Next Session

Bulletin inserts, flyers, letters and e-mails are found on the DVD. You will need to send those for Session 3.

## Social Media Suggestions

Post any of the following memes and discussion sparkers on the parish Facebook page. The memes may also be posted on Pinterest and Twitter. They are found on the DVD (click on "Social Media Resources").

- Upload Meme 2A with this status message: *Where in life have you seen transformation? Have you ever seen it happen in a person? Have you been transformed? If so, how?* **#masstomission**

- Upload Meme 2B with this status message: *The word sacrifice comes from a root word that means "to make holy." What was Jesus' great sacrifice? How are you invited into it? When you think of making yourself a sacrifice, what is your reaction?* **#masstomission**

- Upload Meme 2C with this status message: *God's promised forgiveness is so vast as to be almost unimaginable. Do you believe in it? When you pray for forgiveness in Mass, do you bring your entire self to that prayer? What is your relationship with the Sacrament of Reconciliation?* **#masstomission**

- Upload Meme 2D with this status message: *In the liturgy, we cry out to God for mercy. Think of places where healing is needed, and visualize them the next time you say this prayer. Also, use it this week as a short form of petition, silently, each day.* **#masstomission**

- Upload Meme 2E with this status message: *During Christmas Time, we fill with joy and burst into song (the Gloria), extolling all that God has done for us through the birth of his Son. But this joyful noise is part of every liturgy outside of those in Advent and Lent. As you sing this prayer in Mass, imagine yourself as part of the heavenly choir, and sing as if no one—but our God—is listening!* **#masstomission**

- With their permission, take a picture of a group of the participants and post it on Facebook with this status message: *Just a bunch of happy sinners. Saved.* **#masstomission**

# Chapter Three: The Liturgy of the Word

# Session 3 Outline

## Objectives

- Understand when the Word of God is proclaimed, Christ himself is speaking to us.
- Have a basic understanding of the pattern of the Liturgy of the Word and from where the readings are drawn.
- See silence not as excessive pausing but as an act of openness and receptivity.
- See their engagement with the content of the homily as their personal task and responsibility.

## Preparation Items

- snacks and beverages (pastries, soft drinks, coffee, water)
- hospitality minister(s) to greet people as they arrive
- name tags
- computer, screen, projector
- DVD or Blu-ray player and TV
- Session 3 video
- PowerPoint for Session 3 (show slide #1 as people gather)
- *The Book Thief* (optional movie)
- *Romero* (movie)
- prayer space has been prepared
- ritual binders for opening/closing prayer
- Lectionary #16ABC (shorter form of the Gospel)
- music for prayer
- volunteers for leading music and proclaiming the Gospel
- bell, chime, or sound app
- *From Mass to Mission: Understanding the Mass and Its Significance for Our Christian Life*, chapter three

## Opening Prayer

Be sure to prepare the environment before leading this session. The session leader leads prayer. You will want to find a volunteer to proclaim the reading. Invite a parish cantor (and instrumentalist, if possible) to lead all in an opening song about the Word of God that is familiar to your parishioners. Suggestions are "O Word of God" by Ricky Manalo (OCP), "Christ Be Our Light" by Bernadette Farrell (OCP), "We Come to Live Your Word" by Kate Cuddy (OCP). Make sure enough hymnals or song sheets (be sure to secure proper copyright permission) are in place for all to participate. You may print this page and place it in a ritual binder. The PDF is found on the DVD. Or the reader may use Lectionary #16ABC (the shorter form of the Gospel). Place the binder or Lectionary on a podium before prayer for the reader.

*Invite all to stand and sing the opening song.*

**Leader:** In the name of the Father, † and of the Son, and of the Holy Spirit.

**All:** Amen.

**Reader:** A reading from the holy Gospel according to John.     1:1–5, 9–14

**All:** Glory to you, O Lord.

*All make the Sign of the Cross on their forehead, lips, and heart.*

> In the beginning was the Word, / and the Word was with God, / and the Word was God. / He was in the beginning with God. / All things came to be through him, / and without him nothing came to be. / What came to be through him was life, / and this life was the light of the human race; / the light shines in the darkness, / and the darkness has not overcome it. / The true light, which enlightens everyone, was coming into the world. / He was in the world, / and the world came to be through him, / but the world did not know him. / He came to what was his own, / but his own people did not accept him.
>
> But to those who did accept him he gave power to become children of God, to those who believe in his name, who were born not by natural generation nor by human choice nor by a man's decision but of God. / And the Word became flesh / and made his dwelling among us, / and we saw his glory, / the glory as of the Father's only Son, / full of grace and truth.

**Reader:** The Gospel of the Lord.

**All:** Praise to you Lord Jesus Christ.

*Everyone may be seated. Invite participants to reflect on the Gospel in small groups. Ask: How do you hear Christ speaking to you in the Word? What does the Word teach you about being a Christian? How does hearing the Word help you to act like Christ in the world? Invite the small groups to share with the larger group. Then conclude the opening prayer and reflection with the payer below.*

**Leader:** Lord Jesus,
we believe you are the Word made flesh
who dwelt among us.
In our time together,
bring us to a deeper understanding of you
and the power of your Word.
Who live and reign for ever.

**All:** Amen.

**Leader:** In the name of the Father, † and of the Son, and of the Holy Spirit.

**All:** Amen.

# Discussions and Reflections

## Reaction to Chapter Three

In small groups, ask participants to share their reactions to chapter three in *From Mass to Mission*. Slide #2 in the PowerPoint for Session 3 includes these discussion sparkers: What struck you? What was new to you? What inspired you? Invite participants to share their reflections with the larger group. Other questions are found in the booklet on page 27.

## Video

Show the video for Session 3. After the video, ask participants to discuss what they learned from the video. Show slide #3. What is your reaction to the ideas presented in the video? Which do you find compelling? Which does your parish live out well in their celebration of the Mass? What areas could be improved?

## The Word of God

Show slide #4 and read this quote from the *Constitution on the Sacred Liturgy*: "[Christ] is present in his word, since it is he himself who speaks when the holy Scriptures are read in the Church" (7).

Show slide #5 and ask participants to discuss in their small groups: When have you heard the Word of God at Mass and had it "speak" to you directly? What do you need to be more open to the Word of God? What does it mean to you to know that it is Christ himself who speaks to you in the Word of God? Invite the smaller group to share with the larger group.

## The Readings

Show slide #6. Walk through the structure of the Liturgy of the Word: the First Reading, the Responsorial Psalm, the Second Reading, the Gospel Acclamation, and the Gospel. Also note the homily, Creed, and Universal Prayer as part of every Liturgy of the Word at Sunday Mass.

## Silence

Silence is an integral part of the Mass. After each of the readings is read, we have a moment to pause and integrate what we have just heard. Ask participants to get in a comfortable position. Explain that you are going to start silence by sounding a small bell or chime (if you don't have one, you can use an app on your phone!). Then, the group will enter into five minutes of silence. Ask them to actively let go of thinking. Bring the group out by sounding the bell a second time. Ask them to share their experience with their small group. Draw out reactions by asking them to raise their hands: Who found this restful? Who had a hard time letting go of thoughts? Who was bored? Who fell asleep? Who found value in the silence? Why?

## The Joy of the Gospel

What we hear in the proclamation of the Gospel are the very words about Christ and the words of Christ. This is why the Gospel is found in a special book called the *Book of the Gospels*, which we enthrone in procession and place on the altar.

Show slides #7 and #8 and read aloud this excerpt from Pope Francis' apostolic exhortation, *Evangelii gaudium* (*The Joy of the Gospel*), 3:

> "I invite all Christians, everywhere, at this very moment, to a renewed personal encounter with Jesus Christ, or at least an openness to letting him encounter them; I ask all of you to do this unfailingly each day. No one should think that this invitation is not meant for him or her, since 'no one is excluded from the joy brought by the Lord.' . . . Let us not flee from the resurrection of Jesus, let us never give up, come what will. May nothing inspire more than his life, which impels us onwards!"

Give adults ten minutes to discuss the excerpt from the *Joy of the Gospel*. Show slide #9 and ask: What is your reaction to the words of the Holy Father? What is your reaction to the idea that the pope is addressing all Christians and not just Catholics? Why do Christians need to be called to attend to the message of the Gospel in our age?

## The Homily

During the homily the priest or deacon breaks open the meaning of the Scripture texts and/or the prayers of the Mass. The homily challenges us to live the Gospel in our lives. Watch the homily scene from the movie *Romero* (Scene: 1 hour and 37 minutes into the film). Tell participants that Oscar Romero was the Archbishop of San Salvador. He spoke against injustice and was assassinated in 1980 while celebrating the Mass. He was recently beatified by Pope Francis (beatification is one step in the process of being declared a saint). Give participants ten minutes to read and reflect on Oscar Romero's last homily. Show slide #10 and ask: Do you pay attention to the homily? Why or why not? How would your experience be if you were to take responsibility from getting at least one thing out of the homily that could be applied in your work? How does the homily impact your life?

## The Creed

Refer to page 25 in the booklet. Reiterate that the Creed is an ancient statement of faith. Professing our faith unites us to those in the past and with the universal Church in the present. Show slide #11 and ask: What difference does it make to you to know that you are connected to and share the faith of more than two thousand years of Christian believers? Why is it important to stand together in our common beliefs? How do you share your most important beliefs with others and still maintain your different approaches and opinions? How do you share in your own unique way to the Church?

## The Universal Prayer

The Universal Prayer or the Prayer of the Faithful is the time when we, the community, present our needs to God for the Church, the world, the oppressed, and the local community. This is an ancient practice and is the responsibility of the baptized. What we pray for reveals who we are and what we're committed to.

Show slide #12. Ask each small group to grapple with these questions: What is revealed about your faith community in this Universal Prayer? What values do they express? What issues would your generation pray about each week? Invite small groups to share with the larger group.

## Optional Movie

If your session is taking place within a longer retreat, you might consider showing the movie, *The Book Thief* (PG-13) followed by large group discussion. This powerful film set in World War II Germany is about a young girl who turns to reading for comfort and hope. The plot addresses themes of loss and abandonment, as well as the power of love and trust. This movie should provoke a great conversation about the power of community, the precious gift of the written word, loyalty, and love. Consider showing this movie during a retreat setting.

## Preparing for the Next Session

This week when you go to Mass, listen attentively to the readings, the Gospel, and the homily. Share your reactions with a family member or friend. Point to page 18 in the booklet and stress the importance of preparing to hear the readings at Mass by incorporating them into your daily prayer or reading and reflecting upon the readings beforehand. Ask participants to read chapter four in *From Mass to Mission* and to reflect on the questions on pages 36 and 41. Tell participants to check out the parish Facebook page for an online discussion (see below under Social Media Suggestions).

## Closing Prayer

Pray the Creed together. If participants need the words, it begins on slide #13 in the PowerPoint for Session 3. It is also found in the PDF for the opening and closing prayer for Session 3.

## Advertising the Next Session

Bulletin inserts, flyers, letters and e-mails are found on the DVD. You will need to send those for Session 4.

## Social Media Suggestions

Post any of the following memes and discussion sparkers on the parish Facebook page. The memes may also be posted on Pinterest and Twitter. They are found on the DVD (click on "Social Media Resources").

- Upload Meme 3A with this status message: *To be a Catholic Christian is to be profoundly engaged with all of humanity. Where do you see grief? Anguish? Affliction? What part can you play in contributing to alleviating these and other hardships? How does the Gospel of Jesus Christ inspire you to do so?* **#masstomission**

- Upload Meme 3B with this status message: *For a long time, Catholics felt distant from the Bible. No longer! Take out your Bible and spend some time with it this week. What draws you in?* **#masstomission**

- Upload Meme 3C with this status message: *There is a saying about prayer that goes, "From your mouth to God's ear!" The reverse is also true. How open are you to hearing what God has to say? This week, listen to how the Spirit speaks to you in others, and also open yourself up in a new, deeper way to what is proclaimed in the Liturgy of the Word. What do you hear?* **#masstomission**

# Chapter Four: The Liturgy of the Eucharist

## Session 4 Outline

### Objectives

- ❖ Understand the parts of the Liturgy of the Eucharist, particularly the consecration and words of Institution, and reception of Holy Communion.
- ❖ See the Preparation of the Gifts as a participation in the sacrifice of Christ and tithing as the responsibility of fully initiated Catholics.
- ❖ Connect the Eucharist with thanksgiving and gratitude.
- ❖ Realize that opening up to the gift of the Eucharist is opening up to being changed to be like Christ.

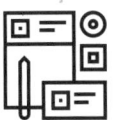

### Preparation Items

- snacks and beverages (pastries, soft drinks, coffee, water)
- hospitality minister(s) to greet people as they arrive
- name tags
- computer, screen, and projector
- DVD or Blu-ray player and TV
- Session 4 video
- PowerPoint for Session 4 (show slide #1 as people gather)
- *Joyeux Noel* (optional movie)
- prayer space has been prepared
- ritual binders for opening / closing prayer
- Lectionary #274 (Weekday) for the Gospel reading
- music for prayer
- volunteers for leading music and proclaiming the Gospel
- hymnals or song sheets for the opening song
- volunteers for leading prayer, leading music, and proclaiming the Gospel
- Bibles
- sign-up sheets for parish ministries
- Representatives from parish ministries
- globe or map of the world for the closing prayer
- *From Mass to Mission: Understanding the Mass and Its Significance for Our Christian Life,* chapter four

### Opening Prayer

Be sure to prepare the environment before leading this session. The session leader leads prayer. You will want to find a volunteer to proclaim the reading. Invite a parish

15

cantor (and instrumentalist, if possible) to lead all in an opening song that is familiar to your parishioners. Suggestions are "Share Your Bread with the Hungry" by David Haas (GIA), "The Supper of the Lord" by Laurence Rosania (OCP), or "In Remembrance of You" by Paul Tate (WLP). Make sure enough hymnals or song sheets (be sure to secure proper copyright permission) are in place for all to participate. You might consider printing the PDF of this opening prayer found on the DVD and place in a ritual binder for both the leader and the reader. Or the reader may use Lectionary #274 (Weekday). Place the binder or Lectionary on a podium before prayer for the reader.

*Invite all to stand and sing the opening song.*

**Leader:** In the name of the Father, † and of the Son, and of the Holy Spirit.

**All:** Amen.

**Reader:** A reading from the holy Gospel according to John. 6:30–35

**All:** Glory to you, O Lord.

*All make the Sign of the Cross on their forehead, lips, and heart.*

> The crowd said to Jesus: "What sign can you do, that we may see and believe in you? What can you do? Our ancestors ate manna in the desert, as it is written:
>
> *'He gave them bread from heaven to eat.'"*
>
> So Jesus said to them, "Amen, amen, I say to you, it was not Moses who gave the bread from heaven; my Father gives you the true bread from heaven. For the bread of God is that which comes down from heaven and gives life to the world."
>
> So they said to Jesus, "Sir, give us this bread always." Jesus said to them, "I am the bread of life; whoever comes to me will never hunger, and whoever believes in me will never thirst."

**Reader:** The Gospel of the Lord.

**All:** Praise to you Lord Jesus Christ.

*Everyone may be seated. Invite participants to reflect on the Gospel in small groups. Ask: How does Christ fill your every need in the Eucharist? What does the Eucharist mean to you? Why is it important for you to receive the Eucharist? Does the Eucharist change you? Why or why not?*

**Leader:** Lord Jesus,
you promised that we would receive you, the Bread of Life.
Help us to deepen our understanding of that great gift,
and help us become people of gratitude and action.
Who live and reign for ever.

**All:** Amen.

**Leader:** In the name of the Father, † and of the Son, and of the Holy Spirit.

**All:** Amen.

## Discussions and Reflections

### Reflection on Chapter Four

In small groups, ask participants to share their reactions to chapter four in *From Mass to Mission*. Slide #2 in the Power Point for Session 4 includes these discussion sparkers: What struck you? What was new to you? What inspired you? Invite participants to share their reflections with the larger group. Other questions are found in the booklet on pages 36 and 41.

### Video

Play the video for Session 4. Invite small group discussion following the video. Show slide #3 and ask: What is your reaction to the ideas presented in the video? Which do you find compelling? Which does your parish live out well in their celebration of the Mass? What areas could be improved? Smaller groups should be encouraged to share with the larger group.

## Preparation of the Gifts

Show slide #4 and restate the purpose of the Preparation of the Gifts. Say: The bread and wine are processed through the assembly by members of the community and are presented to the priest or deacon. Then, a monetary collection is taken by the parish. Show slide #5 and ask: When your parish community collects the offering, who in your household contributes? When should someone participate in making an offering? How old should they be? How much should they give?

Show slide #6. Invite small group discussion on these questions: What do you give? Why? Given what you've learned, are you inclined to give more? Less? Why? How do they participate in the works of justice the community performs? How is your giving tied to works of mercy?

Consider inviting a few representatives from parish ministries (both liturgical and service oriented) to talk to the group about what it means for them to serve. Bring sign-up sheets to this session inviting participants to connect more with the ministries of your community.

## Eucharist Is an Act of Gratitude

Show slide #7. *Eucharist* means "to give thanks." There are days we come to Mass, and even though we intellectually know it's about giving thanks, we don't feel particularly grateful. But gratitude is not just a feeling, it's a form of action and outlook upon life. Recent research from the American Psychological Association shows that the more grateful participants are, the happier and more hopeful they are. Being grateful gives life more meaning, and makes life more satisfying, the study revealed. Show slide #8. In their small groups, have the participants address the question "What are you grateful for?" Have each person write a "gratitude list." Start each sentence with, "I'm grateful for . . ." or "I'm grateful that . . ." Or, have the participants create a gratitude list with their small group. What do you, together, feel thankful for? Share with the larger group.

## The Institution Narrative

Show slide #9. The Institution narrative in the Mass is directly drawn from the Gospel accounts and Paul's first letter to the Corinthians. Give each group a Bible. Ask them to find the following passages: Luke 22:12–14, Mark 14:22–24, Matthew 26:26–28, John 13:1–15, 1 Corinthians 11:23–26. Show slide #10. Ask participants to read aloud and compare these passages. What is the same? What is different? Which have echoes of the language of the Mass? What do they think of the foot washing account? How is this different than the other accounts of the Last Supper? What does the foot washing reveal about the Eucharist? Share with the larger group.

## Sign of Peace

While the "kiss of peace" began in the second century, it had largely disappeared by the mid-twentieth century. It was reinstituted as an optional part of the Mass after the liturgical reforms that were called for by the Second Vatican Council were implemented. When we offer each other a sign of Christ's peace, we are acknowledging the communion, charity, and peace that should characterize our lives together as Christians. We cannot worship God in "Spirit and truth" (John 4:23) if we are harboring grudges, resentment or, even worse, hatred. Show slide #11. Ask adults to respond to the following questions in their small groups: How do you relate to the Sign of Peace? Do you embrace it or resist it? Do you radiate warmth or do people sense you are participating begrudgingly? Are you generous to all your family members as you share the peace, or do you use it to underscore distance or resentment you are feeling? Share with the larger group.

## Receiving Communion

Reiterate what it means to receive Communion. Show slides #12, #13, and #14 and say: Listen to this teaching from St. Augustine (read this aloud and slowly):

> "What is seen is a mere physical likeness; what is grasped bears spiritual fruit. So now, if you want to understand the body of Christ, listen to the Apostle Paul speaking to the faithful: 'You are the body of

Christ, member for member' (1 Corinthians 12:27). If you, therefore, are Christ's body and members, it is your own mystery that is placed on the Lord's table! It is your own mystery that you are receiving! You are saying 'Amen' to what you are: your response is a personal signature, affirming your faith. When you hear 'The body of Christ.' you reply 'Amen.' Be a member of Christ's body, then, so that your 'Amen' may ring true! But what role does the bread play? We have no theory of our own to propose here; listen, instead, to what Paul says about this sacrament: 'The bread is one, and we, though many, are one body' (1 Corinthians 10:17). Understand and rejoice: unity, truth, faithfulness, love. 'One bread,' he says. What is this one bread? Is it not the 'one body,' formed from many? Remember: bread doesn't come from a single grain, but from many. When you received exorcism, you were 'ground.' When you were baptized, you were 'leavened.' When you received the fire of the Holy Spirit, you were 'baked.' Be what you see; receive what you are."

Show slide #15 and ask: What do you think of St. Augustine's idea that YOU are what is on the table at the Eucharist? What does it mean to "be what you see; receive what you are?" How do you think this relates to Mass and how Mass is connected to how we act in the world? Show slide #16 and ask: How does "being what you receive" relate to Mass and how Mass is connected to how we act in the world? How does receiving the Eucharist change you?

## Optional Movie

If your session is taking place within a longer retreat, you might consider showing the movie, *Joyeux Noel* (PG-13) followed by large group discussion. This is a French movie about the truce that occurred between French, Scottish, and German soldiers on Christmas Eve of 1914 on a battlefield. What role does religion play in this movie? How does their shared experience of Christianity challenge the men involved? What do you make of Fr. Palmer's choice to say Mass in this setting? What is your reaction to what happens to the men as soldiers after they have come to know each other? How is the power of the Eucharist part of this movie?

## Preparing for the Next Session

As mentioned in the first session, we are encouraged to generate full, conscious, and active participation in the liturgy. Ask the participants to see if they can do this the next time they are at Mass. Encourage them to pray more fully or to simply participate more generously—such as donating to the collection, listening attentively and joining with the sung responses to the Eucharistic Prayer, giving the Sign of Peace more genuinely to those around them, singing the Communion song, and staying until the dismissal at the end of Mass. Participants may also reflect on the questions found on page 45 in their booklet. Ask them to bring their reflections to the next session and read chapter five in *From Mass to Mission*.

## Closing Prayer

*Place a globe or a map of the world in a central spot and gather the participants around it. Pray the following prayer:*

**Leader:** Jesus, you said to your followers,
peace I give to you, my peace I leave you.
Tonight we think of all the places in the world
that are suffering from war, violence,
and disruption.
We ask you, the Prince of Peace,
to shower your grace on our homes,
our community,
our parish of **N.**, our state, our nation,
and our world.
For whom should we pray today (tonight)?
Please say your place or situation out loud.

*[Leaders should now model the process, for example saying, "I pray for peace in Syria and comfort for the thousands of displaced men, women, and children." Allow participants to share and allow silence if needed for*

*people to start and continue this prayer.] Conclude with the prayer on page 27.*

**Leader:** Christ our brother,
we follow you and ask you to
make us peacemakers.
Journey with us into our lives this week
and make your presence known in each of us.
Who live and reign for ever.

**All:** Amen.

**Leader:** Let us close by offering each other a sign of Christ's peace.

*Give participants a few minutes to offer the Sign of Peace. You might wish to dismiss people with "Go in peace."*

## Advertising the Next Session

Bulletin inserts, flyers, letters, and e-mails are found on the DVD. You will need to send those for Session 5.

## Social Media Suggestions

Post any of the following memes and discussion sparkers on the parish Facebook page. The memes may also be posted on Pinterest and Twitter. They are found on the DVD (click on "Social Media Resources").

- Upload Meme 4A with this status message: *One of the most popular songs of the past fifty years was "Let There Be Peace on Earth." Bring the lyrics to mind, or find them in a songbook or on the Internet. For how long has humanity longed for peace? Where is peace needed in the world right now? Pray for peace today. Comment below about the need for peace.* #masstomission

- Upload Meme 4B with this status message: *Christ give himself to us in the most humble yet essential form known to humankind: bread. Think about the countless forms bread takes, from flatbreads to yeast breads to delicious sweet breads. Take a few minutes and truly savor a piece of your favorite bread. What does this teach you about the Eucharist?* #masstomission

- Upload Meme 4C with this status message: *Christ's sacrifice was once and for all time, and it is made present again every time we experience the Eucharistic liturgy. We implore God to make "us an eternal offering," as well. At that moment, do you place yourself on the altar, purified of sin and pleasing to God? Why or why not?* #masstomission

- Upload Meme 4D with this status message: *The Trinity is one of the great mysteries of our faith. We pray to God the Father through Christ in the liturgy, and we invite the Holy Spirit to come upon us and upon the gifts we have prepared with our priest celebrant. "We are one body, one Spirit in Christ." How do you see the Holy Spirit as the source of our unity?* #masstomission

- Upload Meme 4E with this status message: *The Sign of Peace is an ancient practice, a demonstration of the depth of our love for each other and that we have received the peace that Christ has given to us. What are your feelings about the Sign of Peace? Excited? Resistant? Do you feel engaged? Awkward? Pray to have God expand your experience this week.* #masstomission

- Post a picture of your parish community at Mass with this status message: *Banquet. No bad seats. You're invited.* #masstomission

# Chapter Five:
# The Concluding Rites and Our Call to Mission

# Session 5 Outline

##  Objectives for Session 5

- Understand that Mass is connected to mission.
- See blessing as an act of God's grace, not merely words spoken.
- Begin to think about how we can live as people of justice, fed and fueled by Christ's presence in the Mass.

## 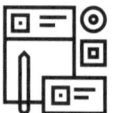 Preparation Items

- snacks and beverages (pastries, soft drinks, coffee, water)
- hospitality minister(s) to greet people as they arrive
- name tags
- computer, screen, and projector
- DVD or Blu-ray player and TV
- Session 5 video
- PowerPoint for Session 5 (show slide #1 as people gather)
- *Amazing Grace* (optional movie)
- prayer space has been prepared
- ritual binders for opening/closing prayer
- Lectionary #102C for the Gospel reading (shorter form)
- music for prayer
- volunteers for leading music and proclaiming the Gospel
- hymnals or song sheets for the opening song
- copies of the parish bulletin and local newspaper
- bowl with blessed water
- *From Mass to Mission: Understanding the Mass and Its Significance for Our Christian Life,* chapter five

##  Opening Prayer

Be sure to prepare the environment before leading this session. The session leader leads prayer. You will want to find a volunteer to proclaim the reading. Invite a parish cantor (and instrumentalist, if possible) to lead all in an opening song about mission that is familiar to your parishioners. Suggestions are "We Will Serve the Lord" by Rory Cooney (GIA Publications), "We Are Called" by David Haas (GIA Publications), "Lead Me, Lord" by John Becker (OCP), or "Go to the World!" by Sylvia G. Dunstan (SINE NOMINE). Make sure enough hymnals or song sheets (be sure to secure proper copyright permission) are in place for all to participate. You might consider printing the PDF of this opening prayer found on the DVD and place it in a ritual binder for both the leader and the reader. Or the reader may use Lectionary #102C (the shorter form of the Gospel). Place the binder or Lectionary on a podium before prayer for the reader.

*Invite all to stand and sing the opening song.*

**Leader:** In the name of the Father, † and of the Son, and of the Holy Spirit.

**All:** Amen.

**Reader:** A reading from the holy Gospel according to Luke.  *10:1–9*

**All:** Glory to you, O Lord.

*All make the Sign of the Cross on their forehead, lips, and heart.*

> At that time the Lord appointed seventy-two others whom he sent ahead of him in pairs to every town and place he intended to visit. He said to them, "The harvest is abundant but the laborers are few; so ask the master of the harvest to send out laborers for his harvest. Go on your way; behold, I am sending you like lambs among wolves. Carry no money bag, no sack, no sandals; and greet no one along the way. Into whatever house you enter, first say, 'Peace to this household.' If a peaceful person lives there, your peace will rest on him; but if not, it will return to you. Stay in the same house and eat and drink what is offered to you, for the laborer deserves his payment. Do not move about from one house to another. Whatever town you enter and they welcome you, eat what is set before you, cure the sick in it and say to them, 'The kingdom of God is at hand for you.'"

**Reader:** The Gospel of the Lord.

**All:** Praise to you, Lord Jesus Christ.

*Everyone may be seated. Invite participants to reflect on the Gospel in small groups. Ask: How do you help bring forth the Kingdom of God? How does participating at Mass help you do this? Invite the small groups to share* with the larger group. Then conclude the opening prayer and reflection with the payer below.

**Leader:** Lord Jesus,
when we were baptized,
we were joined to you as priest, prophet, and king.
Help us deepen the connection between knowing you
and living your ways,
so that all the world might know your peace.
You live and reign for ever.

**All:** Amen.

**Leader:** In the name of the Father, † and of the Son, and of the Holy Spirit.

**All:** Amen.

## Discussions and Reflections

### Reflection on Chapter Five

In small groups, ask participants to share their reactions to chapter five in *From Mass to Mission*. Slide #2 in the Power Point for Session 5 includes these discussion sparkers: What struck you? What was new to you? What inspired you? Invite participants to share their reflections with the larger group. Other questions are found in the booklet on page 45.

### The Concluding Rites and Video

Show slide #3. Note the purpose of the Concluding Rites. Say: On page 40 in your booklet we read:

> "Before we leave the celebration, we resolve a few final matters. We make connections between the Eucharist we have celebrated and the ministry of the upcoming week. We receive a final blessing. And we hear our commission to bring Christ to the world."

Show the video for Session 5. Invite participants to talk in their small groups about their reaction to the video. Show slide #4 and ask: What is your reaction to the ideas presented in the video? Which do you find compelling? Which does your parish live out well in their celebration of the Mass? What areas could be improved? How well do you live out your call to mission?

## The Sign of the Cross

As he completes the final blessing, the priest makes the Sign of the Cross. This is also how Mass begins. In Baptism, the priest, parents, and godparents trace the Sign of the Cross on the forehead of the one being baptized. Many of us make the Sign of the Cross using holy water when we enter the sanctuary of our Church. The Sign of the Cross is a gesture of blessing, whole and complete in and of itself, and is considered a sacramental or sacred sign. Show slide #5 and ask: When do you make the Sign of the Cross? Share as a group. In your sharing, see if you discover a new time that you might do this.

## Final Blessing and Dismissal

By the end of Mass, we have heard the Word of God and received the Body and Blood of Christ. The community is sent with a blessing. This blessing is not just a bunch of words; we believe that it is an act that generates the reality it evokes. While the priest prays the blessing, it comes from God to his people.

Show slides #6, #7, #8, and #9. Read the quote from St. Gregory. Give participants a few moments to reflect on this quote. Then show slide #10 and ask: When do you leave Mass? Do you stay until it is over? Do you see the final blessing as an important part of the Mass? Why or why not? Do you "follow the way of martyrdom in [your] life," as St. Gregory of Sinai suggested? What would contemporary martyrdom look like in the everyday life of the average Christian? Invite the smaller groups to share with the larger group.

## A Missionary Church

Show slides #11, #12, and #13. Read the quote from Pope Benedict XVI's encyclical letter:

"The love that we celebrate in the sacrament is not something we can keep to ourselves. By its very nature it demands to be shared with all. What the world needs is God's love; it needs to encounter Christ and to believe in him. The Eucharist is thus the source and summit not only of the Church's life, but also of her mission: 'an authentically Eucharistic Church is a missionary Church.' We too must be able to tell our brothers and sisters with conviction: 'That which we have seen and heard we proclaim also to you, so that you may have fellowship with us' (1 John 1:3). Truly, nothing is more beautiful than to know Christ and to make him known to others" (*Sacramentum caritatis*, 84).

Give participants a few moments to reflect on this quote. Then show slide #14 and ask: How are you being called by the Mass to share the love of God with others? What might you have to let go of in order to let that happen more effectively? Invite the smaller groups to share their reflections with the larger group.

## Works of Justice

Show slides #15 and #16. On the World Day of Peace in 2005, Pope St. John Paul II spoke of the Eucharist:

"May [the Church] find in this *supreme sacrament of love* the wellspring of all communion: communion with Jesus the Redeemer and in him, with every human being . . . In a word, by sharing in the one bread and the one cup, we come to recognize one another as brothers and sisters, despite every difference of language, nationality and culture. We come to realize that we are *God's family* and together we can . . . [build] a world based on the values of justice, freedom, and peace."

Give participants a few moments to reflect on this quote. Then distribute a few parish bulletins to each group. Then show slide #17. Ask participants to identify actions of solidarity and justice performed by community members. Which do they find most compelling? Distribute copies of your local paper, as well. What issues are happening in the world that your community could and should be in action on? Why? How does your parish community help to "build a world based on the values of justice, freedom, and peace?" Share in small groups, and then share with the larger group.

## Being the Body of Christ

Show slide #18. The word *Mass* comes from the Latin texts for the final dismissal, *"Ite, missa est."* Literally translated into English, this means "Go, she [the Church] has been sent." This dismissal is tied to mission. We are sent forth to live as disciples of Christ, to live lives that are fruitful. We remember the words of Jesus in the Gospel according to Matthew (show slide #19): "By their fruits you will know them" (Matthew 7:16). Show slide #20. The Church has a threefold duty: we must proclaim Christ to the world, we must worship him in spirit and truth, and we must carry him to the world in acts of humble service. These principles have always been part of our communal life. Show slide #21. This is reflected in one of the four options the Church provides for the final dismissal that is said by the priest or deacon: "Go in peace, glorifying the Lord by your life."

Show slide #22. In small groups, discuss: What is one action you could take in the upcoming week to glorify the Lord with their life? Give them at least three minutes of silence to dwell on this question. Share in small groups, and then with the larger group.

## Optional Movie

If your session is taking place within a longer retreat, you might consider showing the movie, *Amazing Grace* (PG) followed by large group discussion. This movie is a true story about the life of William Wilberforce and powerfully demonstrates both the cost and the fruit of discipleship. William Wilberforce almost singlehandedly led the drive to end the British Slave Trade. After showing the movie ask: In what ways is Christianity central to William's story? What moments were pivotal in his journey? How did William generate partnerships to achieve his end? What did this effort cost William? What did he gain?

## Concluding Remarks

Show slide #23. Say: At Mass, be attentive to the moment the priest pours the water into the wine. Visualize the gift of yourself that you are placing in union with Christ's gift. As the priest prepares the gifts, ask God to prepare you to receive him and to empower you to live your discipleship. Mass is about offering ourselves as well as the bread and wine. Show slide #24 and say: This week, think about these questions. What would it mean for you to offer yourself to God? Can you imagine surrendering to God all that concerns you, your stresses and challenges? Can you imagine giving God your struggles or weaknesses? Your joys and hopes?

## Closing Prayer

*You may print this page and place in a ritual binder. The PDF is found on the DVD.*

*Place a bowl of blessed water in the center of the group. Place it on a table that is draped in a colored cloth (use the color of the liturgical season).*

*Let us pray. (All for a moment of silent prayer.)*

**Leader:** Heavenly Father,
 you have provided us with all that is good.
 Be with us in all that we do
 and help us make good decisions about the paths we will take.
 Help us face struggles with friends and family and in our neighborhoods.
 Provide us with the patience to solve conflicts peacefully.
 Grant us prudence when faced with temptation.
 Guide us as we navigate the twists and turns of our lives.
 Keep us mindful to be attentive as we live out our baptismal promise to serve you.

Bless us, Lord, and help us to be kind
  to one another.
Through our Lord Jesus Christ your Son,
who lives and reigns with you
  in the unity of the Holy Spirit,
one God, for ever and ever.

**All:** Amen.

*Allow for a moment of silent reflection.*

*Invite participants to bless each other while a musician sings "Be Thou My Vision" (or another suitable song about mission or renewing baptismal promises).*

**Leader:** Let us now bless each other with holy water as we complete our time of learning and return to the mission of God's Kingdom.

## Social Media Suggestions

Post any of the following memes and discussion sparkers on the parish Facebook page. The memes may also be posted on Pinterest and Twitter. They are found on the DVD (click on "Social Media Resources").

- Upload Meme 5A with this status message: *Jesus sent the Apostles into the world two by two. At Pentecost, the Holy Spirit came upon them, enabling them to reach out beyond their small circle to the entire world. Do you see yourself as being part of Christ's mission? How do you participate? Could you contribute more?* #masstomission

- Upload Meme 5B with this status message: *Often, people head out the church doors after they have received Communion. The announcements and bulletin reveal to us how our community is living its individual discipleship and collective call to holiness. If you thought of the parish announcements as prayer, would you listen to them differently?* #masstomission

- Upload Meme 5C with this status message: *To be given a commission is usually an honor. We are commissioned by Christ through the sacraments of initiation and in our weekly (or daily) Eucharist received at Mass. What have you been gifted with? What have you been gifted for?* #masstomission

- Upload Meme 5D with this status message: *When our parish sings a closing song, it ends our time of prayer with themes of discipleship, mission, and challenges us to live the Gospel in our daily lives. This week, pay close attention to the last song at Mass. What does it tell you? How can you live its vision?* #masstomission

- Upload Meme 5E with this status message: *Going to Mass is not complete as we leave the pew. Our job is to live the Gospel in the days ahead to the best of our ability, trusting that we have been gifted with everything we need to do so, and to do so very well. Where do you find yourself in life? Can you imagine, through words or actions, how you might proclaim the Gospel in those places?* #masstomission

- Post a picture of the people in your parish serving others in some way with this status message: *Got purpose?* #masstomission